Preface: "I am just a Chill Guy"

Hey, I'm Nivaan Alex, and I'm 12 years old. This book you're about to dive into was inspired by something pretty simple—the Chill Guy meme. You know the one? It was all over my YouTube Shorts feed, popping up every few minutes while I was scrolling like every other teen. At first, I just laughed it off, but then it started to hit me differently. I started thinking, "What if I actually lived like that? What if I could be a 'Chill Guy'?" That idea stuck with me and made me rethink a lot of things. I realized that living a calm, laid-back life could actually make everything feel a little easier, a little more fun, and a lot less stressful. So, I decided to write this book on The Art of Chilling. It's about how to live a chilled-out life, not just when you're kicking back, but in everything you do. If you're ready to kick stress to the curb and embrace a more relaxed, balanced way of living, this book is for you. Let's figure out how to be that person—the one who's always cool, collected, and living their best, most chill life.

Prologue: Chill Like a Pro (Without Even Trying Too Hard)

Sup! So you decided to pick up this book, huh? Magnificent choice. If you're somewhat like me, life sometimes is just too much. Between school, friends, family, and trying to figure out why everyone on social media looks like they have their lives together, it's easy to feel like you're carrying the weight of the world on your shoulders. Guess what? You don't have to.

That's right. You can actually learn to live your life without stressing over every little thing. You can stop overthinking, let go of the stuff that doesn't matter, and start having a good time, even when things aren't perfect. The secret? It's all about mastering the art of chill.

Now, before you think, "Oh great, here's another lecture about being perfect," let me tell you this: being chill isn't about pretending everything's fine or acting like you don't care about anything. (Because let's be real, even the most chill people care about stuff—they just don't let it ruin their day.) Being chill is about learning how to handle life's ups and downs without losing your cool. It's about figuring out what really matters and letting go of the rest. And guess what? It's not as hard as it sounds.

Chapter 1: Why Chill Matters?

Picture this: You're at school, and you just tripped in the hallway. Your books are everywhere, people are staring, and someone even giggles. What's your first reaction? Are you dying of embarrassment and wishing the ground would swallow you whole? Or are you laughing it off and saying, "Guess I'm practicing my gymnastics skills!" Here's the thing: embarrassing stuff happens to everyone. Stressful situations? Totally normal. But how you handle them makes all the difference. If you let every little thing ruin your mood, you're going to spend your whole life feeling like a human stress ball. That's exhausting, right?

Being chill isn't about avoiding bad stuff. It's about deciding that the bad stuff doesn't get to control your mood, your day, or your life. It's about being the kind of person who says, "Yeah, that was awkward, but I'm good," and then moves on like a boss.

Chapter 2: Who Can Be Chill? (Spoiler: You Can)

You might be thinking, "Okay, but I'm not naturally a chill person. I'm always overthinking, worrying, or stressing out." Guess what? That's totally fine. Being chill isn't something you're born with—it's something you learn. Think of it like learning to ride a bike. At first, it feels weird and wobbly, and you're pretty sure you're going to crash. But the more you practice, the easier it gets. And before you know it, you're cruising down the street, wind in your hair, feeling like the coolest person ever.

Learning to be chill works the same way. You start with small steps—like laughing at yourself when you mess up or taking a deep breath instead of freaking out. Over time, those little habits add up, and suddenly, you're the kind of person who can handle anything life throws at you without breaking a sweat.

Chapter 3: What This Book is (And What It's Not)

Let's get one thing straight: this book is not about turning you into a meditation master or some kind of Zen guru. If you want to sit cross-legged on a mountain and chant "om" for hours, cool. But that's not what we're doing here. This book is about real-life chill. The kind of chill you can use when your sibling steals your stuff, or your teacher gives you a surprise quiz, or your best friend cancels plans at the last minute. It's about learning simple, no-nonsense ways to stay calm, let go of dumb stuff, and enjoy life more—even when it's messy.

Here's what you'll find in these pages: Relatable advice: Because nobody has time for complicated, boring tips that don't work. Real talk: I'll tell you what works and what doesn't, without all the fake positivity. Actionable steps: Each chapter has simple, practical tips you can actually use to make life less stressful and more fun. A little humor: Because let's face it—laughing makes everything easier.

So, are you ready to ditch the stress and embrace the chill? Are you ready to handle life's chaos like the pro I know you can be? If so, let's dive in. The Art of Chill isn't just a book—it's your new way of looking at life. Let's do this!

Chapter 4: Chill? What's That?

Alright, let's get one thing straight: being chill isn't about being lazy or pretending like you don't care about anything. Nah, that's not it. Being chill is like having a superpower that helps you deal with life without freaking out over every little thing. Imagine walking into class after forgetting your homework and not immediately wanting to dig a hole and hide in it forever. Instead, you're like, "Okay, it happens. What's next?" That's the vibe we're going for. Let's dive in and figure out what being chill actually means, why stressing out is the worst, and how being chill can seriously make your life way better.

Chapter 5: What Does Being Chill Even Mean?

Being chill is all about staying calm, even when things get messy. It's like being on a rollercoaster—sure, there are ups and downs, but instead of screaming your head off at every drop, you're just enjoying the ride (or at least pretending to). It doesn't mean you're ignoring problems or acting like nothing ever bothers you. It's more about not letting the stuff you can't control ruin your whole day. Think of the chillest person you know. Maybe it's that kid in your class who always seems relaxed, even when there's a surprise test, or your cousin who laughs off awkward moments like they're no big deal. What makes them different? They've figured out that stressing out doesn't fix anything. They don't let little annoyances like spilling a drink or getting stuck in traffic mess with their mood. They just roll with it. That's what being chill is all about—rolling with the punches and not letting every bump in the road feel like the end of the world.

Being chill also means not taking yourself too seriously. If you trip in the hallway, being chill means laughing it off instead of panicking about who saw you. It's knowing that everyone messes up sometimes, and it's really not a big deal. People who are chill don't waste time worrying about what others think. They focus on what makes them happy and let the rest slide.

Chapter 6: Why Stress is Lame

Stress is like that annoying fly buzzing around your room—it's small, but it can ruin everything if you let it. Think about the last time you were super stressed. Maybe it was a big test, a fight with your friend, or your parents nagging you about cleaning your room (ugh). Did stressing out actually help? Probably not. Most of the time, stress just makes everything feel worse. It's like piling extra weight onto a backpack that's already too heavy. And what's the point of that?

When you're stressed, your brain goes into overdrive. It starts running through every possible "what if" scenario, even the ridiculous ones. "What if I fail this test and never get into college and end up living in my parents' basement forever?" Chill people know how to shut that down. They remind themselves that stressing doesn't change anything. If you can't control something, why waste your energy worrying about it? And if you can control it, then just do what you need to do and move on.

Another reason stress is lame? It totally messes with your vibe. When you're stressed, you're more likely to snap at people, make dumb mistakes, or feel like you're stuck in a bad mood all day. It's like a chain reaction that turns one bad moment into a bad day. Being chill breaks that chain. Instead of letting one little thing ruin everything, you learn to shrug it off and keep going.

Chapter 7: How Being Chill Can Make Life Way Better

Okay, so we know stress is the worst. But what's so great about being chill? First of all, being chill makes you way more fun to be around. Nobody wants to hang out with someone who's always freaking out or complaining about stuff. Chill people have this magnetic energy that makes everyone feel comfortable. They're the ones who can turn an awkward moment into a joke or make a boring day feel exciting just by being themselves.

Being chill also makes life way easier. Think about it—if you're not constantly stressing, you have way more time and energy to focus on the good stuff. You're not wasting hours replaying embarrassing moments in your head or worrying about things that might not even happen. Instead, you're enjoying the moment and finding ways to make the best out of every situation.

Another cool thing about being chill? It helps you bounce back faster when things go wrong. Let's say you bomb a test or get into a fight with your best friend. A stressed-out person might spend days or even weeks feeling upset about it. But a chill person? They'll take a deep breath, figure out what they can do to fix it, and then move on. They don't let one bad moment define them.

Finally, being chill just feels good. When you're not constantly stressed, you sleep better, laugh more, and actually enjoy life. You start to notice all the little things that make life awesome, like a funny meme, a sunny day, or your favorite snack. And honestly, isn't that what life's all about?

So, if you're ready to stop stressing and start living your best, chillest life, you're in the right place. Let's keep going and figure out how to master the art of chill, one step at a time.

Chapter 8: Stress Monsters and How to Defeat Them

Stress is an inevitable part of life. It's something we all experience, whether we're juggling work deadlines, navigating personal relationships, or dealing with unexpected challenges. However, stress doesn't just leave a lasting impact on our emotional well-being—it also wreaks havoc on our brains, influencing how we think, feel, and behave. The good news is that by understanding how stress works and taking active steps to manage it, we can reduce its impact and regain control over our lives. In this section, we'll explore what stress does to your brain, how to stay calm when things go wrong, and how to spot stress before it overwhelms you.

Chapter 9: What Stress Does to Your Brain (It's Not Pretty)

Stress, in small doses, can actually be beneficial. It motivates us to take action and stay alert in the face of challenges. However, chronic or excessive stress is a different story. When stress becomes prolonged, it starts to take a serious toll on both our mental and physical health.

The brain plays a central role in how we experience stress. When you're stressed, your brain activates the body's "fight-or-flight" response, which releases a cocktail of stress hormones, including cortisol and adrenaline. These hormones prepare the body to face danger by increasing heart rate, blood pressure, and energy levels. While this response is useful in life-threatening situations, it's not designed to be sustained over long periods of time. In the modern world, most stressors—such as work pressure or financial strain—are not immediately life-threatening, but our brains don't distinguish between "real" threats and everyday stressors.

Chronic stress can lead to lasting changes in the brain. For instance, prolonged exposure to high levels of cortisol can shrink the hippocampus, a brain area critical for memory and learning. This may contribute to difficulties in concentration, forgetfulness, and cognitive decline. Moreover, the amygdala, the part of the brain responsible for emotions like fear and anxiety, can become hyperactive under prolonged stress, leading to heightened feelings of anxiety and irritability.

Not only does stress affect brain structure and function, but it also impacts our emotional regulation. The prefrontal cortex, which governs decision-making and impulse control, can become less active when you're stressed, impairing your ability to think clearly and make thoughtful decisions. This can result in poor judgment, rash behavior, and difficulty managing emotions.

In essence, chronic stress can make us feel like we're constantly in "survival mode," and the long-term consequences of this can be both mentally and physically draining. The key is to understand these effects so we can better manage stress before it takes over.

Chapter 10: The Secret to Staying Calm When Stuff Goes Wrong

It's easy to feel overwhelmed when life takes an unexpected turn. Maybe you receive some bad news, a project falls behind schedule, or a personal situation causes distress. In those moments, your brain may be flooded with emotions, making it hard to think clearly or stay calm. However, there are strategies you can use to remain calm in the face of adversity.

1. Breathe Deeply: Deep breathing is one of the simplest yet most powerful tools for reducing stress. When you're stressed, your breathing tends to become shallow and rapid, which can further trigger the stress response. Deep, slow breaths help activate the parasympathetic nervous system (also known as the "rest-and-digest" system), which counteracts the fight-or-flight response. The simple act of inhaling deeply and exhaling slowly can calm your mind and restore a sense of control.

2. Focus on the Present Moment: Stress often arises when we get caught up in worrying about the future or ruminating on past events. Practicing mindfulness—paying attention to the present moment without judgment—can help you break this cycle. By focusing on what you can control right now, you reduce the power of your worries and create mental space to think clearly.

3. Reframe the Situation: When something goes wrong, it's easy to interpret it as a catastrophe. However, by consciously reframing the situation, you can view it from a different perspective. For example, instead of thinking, "This is a disaster," try telling yourself, "This is a challenge, but I can handle it." This shift in mindset can help you approach problems more calmly and with a greater sense of control.

4. Take a Break: Sometimes, the best way to stay calm is to remove yourself from a stressful situation for a short period of time. Taking a walk, practicing some yoga, or simply sitting quietly for a few minutes can give your mind a chance to reset. In these moments, you're giving yourself the space to reflect, recharge, and come back to the situation with a clearer head.

By using these strategies, you can cultivate a sense of calm even in the midst of chaos. The goal isn't to eliminate stress completely, but to manage it effectively so that it doesn't derail your well-being.

Chapter 11: How to Spot Stress Before It Takes Over

Stress can sneak up on you. Often, we don't realize we're becoming overwhelmed until it's too late, and by then, the effects of stress may have already started to take a toll on our bodies and minds. The key to managing stress is being able to spot the early warning signs before they escalate into something more serious.

Some common physical signs of stress include:

- Tension in your muscles (especially in the neck, shoulders, and jaw)

- Headaches or migraines

- Digestive issues, such as stomachaches, constipation, or diarrhea

- Increased heart rate or a feeling of "fluttering" in the chest

- Fatigue, even after a full night's rest

In addition to physical symptoms, stress can manifest emotionally and mentally. You may notice:

- Irritability or a short temper

- Difficulty concentrating or making decisions

- Mood swings, including feelings of sadness or anxiety

- Increased worry or a sense of dread about the future

- Feelings of helplessness or being "out of control"

Behaviorally, stress can show up as:

- Procrastination or avoidance of tasks

- Changes in appetite, either overeating or loss of appetite

- Sleep disturbances, such as trouble falling asleep or staying asleep

- Social withdrawal or a tendency to isolate yourself from others

The earlier you can recognize these signs, the better equipped you'll be to take action before stress takes over. Regularly checking in with yourself, both mentally and physically, can help you stay ahead of the curve.

Chapter 12: <u>Starting Your Chill Journey</u>

While stress is a constant presence in modern life, it's also possible to cultivate a sense of calm and resilience. This "chill journey" isn't about eliminating stress entirely, but learning how to stay composed and balanced, no matter what life throws your way. In this section, we'll explore why it's okay to mess up, how to integrate small steps to chill more each day, and how to be chill without appearing indifferent.

Chapter 13: <u>Why It's Okay to Mess Up</u>

One of the most significant sources of stress comes from our fear of failure or making mistakes. We live in a world that often prizes perfectionism, which can create an immense amount of pressure. However, it's important to recognize that mistakes are an inevitable part of life and growth.

Failure is not the end of the world. In fact, it's often through mistakes that we learn the most valuable lessons. Embracing imperfection can actually reduce stress because it takes away the pressure to be flawless. When you allow yourself the freedom to make mistakes, you're giving yourself permission to grow, experiment, and try again.

Being kind to yourself when you mess up is a form of self-compassion. Instead of criticizing yourself or obsessing over what went wrong, treat yourself with the same kindness you would offer a friend in a similar situation. By reframing failure as a learning opportunity, you'll find it easier to let go of the stress and anxiety that often accompany mistakes.

Chapter 14: <u>Small Steps to Chillax More Every Day</u>

Achieving a sense of calm doesn't happen overnight, but with consistent effort, you can gradually build habits that help you stay grounded and chill. Here are some small steps you can take to incorporate more relaxation into your daily routine:

1. Practice Gratitude: Taking time each day to reflect on what you're grateful for can shift your focus away from stress and negativity. Start a gratitude journal and write down three things you're thankful for every day. This simple practice can boost your mood and help you stay more relaxed.

2. Take Mindful Breaks: Throughout the day, give yourself permission to take breaks. Step away from your work, breathe deeply, and check in with your body. Even just a few minutes of mindfulness can lower stress and increase focus.

3. Prioritize Self-Care: Whether it's exercising, cooking a nourishing meal, or reading a good book, make time for activities that replenish your energy and bring you joy. When you take care of your physical and emotional needs, you're better equipped to handle stress.

4. Simplify Your Schedule: Overcommitting to work, social engagements, or personal responsibilities can quickly lead to burnout. Take a look at your calendar and eliminate unnecessary tasks or obligations. Learn to say no when necessary and prioritize the activities that align with your values and well-being.

By implementing these small steps, you'll gradually build resilience against stress and create a more chill, balanced life.

Chapter 15: How to Be Chill Without Acting Like You Don't Care

There's a common misconception that being "chill" means being indifferent or apathetic. In reality, you can be calm and composed while still caring deeply about your goals, relationships, and well-being. The key is in how you respond to challenges and stressors.

Being chill means responding thoughtfully, rather than reacting impulsively. It's about staying grounded in the face of adversity without letting your emotions dictate your behavior.

Chapter 16: Why We Hold Onto Stuff That Doesn't Matter

We all do it. We hold onto stuff — not the physical kind, but emotional and mental baggage. From replaying embarrassing moments in our heads to worrying about things that will never happen, these mental "clutters" weigh us down. But why? Why do we allow these things to stick with us, causing stress, regret, or frustration? Why do we keep obsessing over things that don't matter in the grand scheme of our lives?

Chapter 17: Why It's So Hard to Forget That One Time You Embarrassed Yourself

Think back to a time when you embarrassed yourself. It might have been a slip-up in front of a group, an awkward comment you made in a meeting, or a misstep that still makes you cringe when you remember it. Why does this moment stay with you for so long? It's because of how our brains are wired. Our minds have a tendency to fixate on negative experiences. It's a survival mechanism. Early humans had to remember where dangers were, what could hurt them, or what mistakes could be fatal. Over time, this mechanism became engrained in how we think. In today's world, this survival instinct isn't always helpful; it leads to us replaying embarrassing moments, worrying about past mistakes, or feeling shame over things that, realistically, won't matter in a year — or even next week. Psychologists call this the "negativity bias." It's the idea that we're more likely to remember negative events than positive ones. Evolutionarily speaking, this made sense — remembering dangers kept us alive. But in modern life, this means that we end up overthinking minor mistakes, while ignoring the positives. To make matters worse, we often get caught in a loop of rumination, mentally replaying these moments as if we can change them. Yet, this mental cycle doesn't do anything except drain our emotional energy. What we forget is that most people are so focused on their own worries that they're hardly noticing our mistakes — and if they do, they forget them just as quickly.

Chapter 18: The Truth About "Perfect" People (Hint: They're Not Real)

We all have this image of "perfect" people — the ones who seem to have it all together: flawless appearances, flawless careers, and flawless social lives. The reality, though, is that no one is perfect, despite what Instagram or Pinterest may lead us to believe. In fact, the pursuit of perfection often does more harm than good. First, we need to acknowledge that perfection is a construct, not a reality. Every so-called "perfect" person you admire has flaws, insecurities, and mistakes, even if they're not immediately visible. The people who seem to glide through life effortlessly are probably just better at hiding their struggles, or they've learned to embrace their imperfections. Often, our perception of them as "perfect" has little to do with their actual life experience and more to do with how we measure ourselves against them. When we compare ourselves to this unrealistic ideal, we set ourselves up for disappointment. We end up believing that if we aren't living up to these standards, we are somehow less worthy or less successful. But here's the truth: perfection is unattainable. And in the quest for it, we waste time, energy, and self-compassion that could be better spent on growth, self-love, and self-acceptance. Instead of focusing on the illusion of perfection, it's far more productive to focus on progress, not perfection.

Chapter 19: How Worry is Just Wasted Energy

We often find ourselves spiraling into anxiety about things that might not ever happen. Whether it's worrying about an upcoming presentation, stressing over a social situation, or imagining all the things that could go wrong in our personal lives, worry takes up a lot of mental space. But here's the kicker: worry is essentially wasted energy. Studies show that a large percentage of the things we worry about never happen, and even if they do, the anxiety we experienced beforehand does little to prepare us for it. Worrying is a futile exercise. It keeps us trapped in a cycle of fear and helplessness, preventing us from taking proactive steps or enjoying the present. Yet, we tend to default to worrying because it feels like we are in control. The irony is that the more we worry, the less control we actually have. Instead of spinning our wheels in the endless cycle of "what-ifs," we can choose to redirect that energy into actionable solutions or simply let go. The real power lies in being able to differentiate between what we can control and what we cannot.

Chapter 20: Chill Tricks for Letting Go

Letting go of all the mental clutter, especially the unnecessary stuff, is easier said than done. But it doesn't have to be a painful, complex process. Sometimes, we just need a few tricks up our sleeves to help shift our mindset and release the things that are weighing us down. Here are a few chill methods to get you started.

Chapter 21: How to Laugh It Off (Even When It's Not Funny Yet)

Humor has a magical way of diffusing tension and making even the most uncomfortable situations easier to bear. While it may seem difficult to laugh off something that's really bothering you, a good sense of humor can be one of the most effective ways to let go. The trick is not waiting until you feel "funny" about a situation, but making the conscious choice to laugh even when it's hard. Laughing at your own expense can take the power away from the moment that was causing you stress. It doesn't mean you're belittling yourself; rather, you're choosing not to let the situation control you. By reframing the narrative with humor, you create emotional distance from the event, making it easier to move on. Plus, humor has a way of making you feel lighter, even in the face of adversity. It's one of those life hacks that helps you bounce back quicker and with a more resilient attitude. So, the next time you catch yourself ruminating over a cringe-worthy experience, try to find the humor in it. It's liberating.

Chapter 22: The Power of Saying "Whatever" and Meaning It

There is an unexpected power in the word "whatever." It's not about giving up or being apathetic — it's about choosing not to let things outside of your control consume your thoughts. "Whatever" can be a simple but effective way of acknowledging that certain things just don't matter in the grand scheme of life. That minor inconvenience, that small mistake, or the unimportant opinion of someone else — they don't need to define your emotional state. Saying "whatever" is a reminder that you are not a slave to the little things that try to bog you down. It's an act of releasing unnecessary attachment to things that have no long-term significance. When you start saying "whatever" and meaning it, you'll find that you're less affected by the trivial matters and more present in what truly matters. Letting go doesn't always have to be a grand, emotional process. Sometimes it's as simple as choosing to shrug it off.

Chapter 23: Turning Your Problems Into "Who Cares?" Moments

It's easy to get caught up in the idea that every problem is urgent, that every misstep deserves attention, or that every negative comment is a personal attack. But what if you could change your perspective and turn your problems into "Who cares?" moments? Not every inconvenience, mistake, or slight is worth your energy or time. In fact, most problems are transient and inconsequential when viewed from a broader perspective. Instead of investing emotional capital into things that don't matter, ask yourself, "Who cares?" — and if the answer is "no one," then it's time to let go. Shifting your mindset to one that focuses on the fleeting nature of most problems helps you see that life goes on, no matter how small the issue may seem at the time. Often, we make mountains out of molehills, and by adopting the "Who cares?" approach, we stop making things bigger than they need to be. This mental shift frees up so much unnecessary weight from your shoulders.

Chapter 24: Moving On Like a Pro

Once you start practicing these techniques for letting go, you'll begin to notice a significant change in how you handle life's challenges. But how do you move on from things that have been bothering you for a long time? How do you stop replaying the embarrassing moments, letting go of the past, and fully embracing the present? The following steps can help you move on like a pro.

Chapter 25: How to Stop Replaying Cringe Moments

We've all been there — stuck in the mental loop of replaying a cringe-worthy moment over and over in our minds. Whether it's a social faux pas, an awkward comment, or a failure in front of others, these moments can haunt us. The key to stopping this cycle is realizing that the more you replay the moment, the more power you give it. Instead of giving in to the urge to replay it, consciously choose to redirect your thoughts. One effective technique is to practice mindfulness: when the embarrassing memory pops up, focus on your breath, or on something in your current environment. The goal isn't to suppress the memory, but to prevent it from taking over your thoughts. Over time, with practice, you'll retrain your brain to move past the past, allowing the memory to lose its emotional grip on you.

Chapter 26: Forgetting the Small Stuff (Because It's All Small Stuff)

Life can feel overwhelming when we sweat the small stuff. We get caught up in the details, the tiny mistakes, and the little things that don't actually matter in the long run. But when we take a step back, we realize that most of the things that we stress about are, in fact, insignificant. Whether it's a minor mistake at work, a forgotten appointment, or a mild embarrassment in a social setting.

Chapter 27: Why the Present Rules

There's a common human tendency to either dwell on the past or obsess over the future. The past often feels like it has a magnetic pull, drawing our attention back to mistakes, regrets, or unfinished business. The future, on the other hand, is filled with endless possibilities, which we try to predict or control, usually with worry. But the truth is, both the past and the future are out of our control. The only thing we truly have power over is the present moment, which is why it's crucial to embrace it fully. In this section, we'll explore why living in the present is the key to feeling grounded, happy, and at peace.

Chapter 28: You Can't Time Travel, So Stop Trying

How many times have you wished you could go back in time to undo a mistake or relive a happy moment? Time travel is a fascinating concept, but in reality, it's simply not possible. The past is gone, and no amount of wishing, regretting, or fantasizing about it can change anything. The truth is that time, as we know it, moves in one direction—forward. The more we fixate on the past, the more we miss the present moment. Whether it's replaying an embarrassing conversation or lamenting an opportunity we missed, we essentially waste time and energy on things that cannot be undone. The past only exists in our minds, and it has no bearing on the choices we make today unless we let it. By accepting that we cannot change the past, we free ourselves from unnecessary regret and can start focusing on what's happening now. The present is the only time in which we can make an impact, make choices, and experience life. Once we stop trying to time travel, we can fully engage with the reality before us, and that's where the magic happens.

Chapter 29: Why Worrying About the Future is Pointless

If we can't change the past, we certainly can't predict or control the future. But despite that fact, many of us spend an inordinate amount of time worrying about what might happen. We imagine worst-case scenarios, stress over decisions that haven't yet come to pass, or become paralyzed by the uncertainty of what lies ahead. But here's the kicker: worrying about the future is almost always a waste of time. The majority of things we worry about never even happen, and when they do, the anxiety we spent ahead of time doesn't help us handle them any better. Worrying about an upcoming presentation won't make you more prepared, and stressing about what could go wrong with a relationship won't solve any problems. Instead, it just robs you of the mental energy that could be better spent on the present moment. Anxiety about the future is rooted in the fear of the unknown, but the reality is that the future is unpredictable. No amount of worrying will change that. When we learn to let go of this need for control, we free ourselves to live in the moment, respond to challenges as they come, and trust that things will unfold as they are meant to. When we stop worrying about the future, we create space for peace and clarity in the present.

Chapter 30: Finding Fun in the Stuff You're Already Doing

Many people think that fun is something that must be planned, pursued, or found outside of our routine lives. We wait for vacations, special events, or new experiences to inject excitement into our lives. But the truth is, fun isn't something that's only available on rare occasions. It's something we can find in the present moment, in the things we're already doing. If we stop waiting for external circumstances to make our lives fun, we can start enjoying the everyday activities we often overlook. The way you eat your lunch, the way you talk to a friend, the way you listen to music or take a walk—these can all be fun, but only if you engage with them fully. Fun doesn't have to be extravagant or over-the-top; it's about the attitude with which you approach the activity. If you can approach the simplest tasks with an open mind and a sense of curiosity, you'll find that life is full of opportunities for enjoyment. The key is to stop thinking that fun is something external and start realizing that it's all about how we engage with the world around us. The present moment is already rich with possibilities; we just have to open our eyes and see them.

Chapter 31: How to Be Present Without Falling Asleep

Living in the now doesn't always come naturally, especially in a world filled with distractions. How many times have you found yourself on autopilot, going through the motions of daily life without truly paying attention? Being present requires intentionality—it's about being fully engaged in whatever is happening right in front of you. This section explores how to sharpen your focus, avoid distractions, and stay present in the moment, even when it's easy to zone out.

Chapter 32: The Magic of Paying Attention (Even in Boring Moments)

It's easy to tune out when life feels boring, repetitive, or mundane. When you're stuck in a meeting that doesn't seem relevant, or you're waiting for something to happen, your mind tends to wander. But the truth is, even in these seemingly boring moments, there's magic to be found. The secret to being present is learning to pay attention to the details around you. Whether you're doing dishes, sitting in traffic, or waiting for an appointment, the simple act of paying attention can transform the most mundane moments into something more. When you really focus, you'll notice things you might otherwise miss—the smell of your coffee, the colors of the sky, the sound of the wind rustling in the trees. These small details make up the fabric of the present moment, and by paying attention to them, you ground yourself in the here and now. Even when the task itself seems dull, the act of being fully present can make it feel meaningful. The more you practice paying attention, the more you realize that there's always something worth noticing in any moment. It's not about the activity, it's about the awareness you bring to it.

Chapter 33: How to Stop Multitasking Like You're a Machine

Multitasking has become the norm in our fast-paced society. From juggling work, personal life, and social media, it can feel like you're constantly switching between tasks. But the reality is that multitasking actually hinders your ability to be present. When you split your focus between several things, you end up doing none of them well. The brain isn't designed to handle multiple tasks at once, and when you try to multitask, you're simply moving your attention too quickly between different things. To be present, you have to focus on one thing at a time. This doesn't mean you can't do multiple things in a day, but when you're doing something, be fully immersed in it. If you're working on a project, focus entirely on that. If you're having a conversation, give the other person your full attention. By stopping the habit of multitasking, you create more meaningful connections with the tasks and people around you. It's not about being more efficient; it's about being more engaged. When you focus on one thing at a time, you'll find that the moment becomes richer, and the experience more fulfilling.

Chapter 34: Finding the Good Stuff Around You

Being present is about shifting your focus to the beauty and goodness that already surrounds you. When we're rushing through life, we often overlook the small joys in our daily lives. But when you slow down and look closely, you'll notice that there's a lot to appreciate. Maybe it's the way sunlight streams through your window, or the way your dog greets you with excitement every day, or even just the satisfaction of a warm cup of tea. The present moment is filled with small moments of joy, but only if you're paying attention. Instead of looking for happiness in big events or future achievements, try looking around you right now. There's likely something beautiful in your environment that you've overlooked. By making the effort to notice the good things around you, you create a sense of gratitude and presence that enriches your day-to-day experience. The present is always full of positive moments; it's just a matter of becoming aware of them.

Chapter 35: Chill Hacks for Loving the Moment

Living in the now is a skill that takes practice, but it doesn't have to be complicated. By incorporating a few simple tricks into your routine, you can start loving the present moment more fully. These "chill hacks" help you cultivate an easy-going attitude that lets you embrace the now, even in the middle of a busy life.

Chapter 36: Turn Your Boring Routine into Something Fun

We all have routines that can feel repetitive, from commuting to grocery shopping to cleaning the house. But instead of viewing these activities as chores, try to find a way to make them more enjoyable. You don't have to wait for a special occasion to have fun; you can create fun in your daily routine. For example, make a game out of your cleaning routine, or listen to an audiobook or podcast while doing errands. Find ways to inject some creativity or play into the most mundane tasks, and you'll start to see them in a new light. You'll realize that even the most routine moments can become enjoyable when you approach them with a sense of playfulness. The key is to shift your perspective and make the most of the time you already have, rather than wishing for something more exciting.

Chapter 37: How to Spot Cool Stuff You Miss Every Day

When you're in a hurry, it's easy to overlook the cool, interesting details that make life fun. Whether it's a beautiful flower growing in the sidewalk crack or a funny sign on the street corner, these little moments often pass us by. To be more present, make a conscious effort to slow down and look for the cool things you miss every

Chapter 38: Sharing the Chill Vibes

In a world that often feels fast-paced and full of pressure, sharing a relaxed, laid-back attitude with others can be one of the most powerful things you can do. It's not just about helping yourself stay grounded and calm; it's about spreading those chill vibes to your friends and loved ones. When you help others embrace the present, laugh at their mistakes, and remember that no one is perfect, you create a supportive environment where everyone can just be. Let's explore how to share these easy-going vibes with the people around you.

Chapter 39: How to Help Your Friends Chill Too

The first step to helping your friends chill is leading by example. If you constantly stress about deadlines, overplan every moment, or act like life is one big race, your friends are likely to feel that same pressure. But when you slow down, take things one step at a time, and show that it's okay to breathe and enjoy the moment, you give them permission to do the same. Be the person who laughs off small mistakes and doesn't get caught up in trivial details. Encourage your friends to be present, whether you're hanging out, working, or just chatting. Remind them that it's okay to pause, enjoy the little things, and not take life so seriously. If they feel like they're in a judgment-free zone where it's okay to relax, they'll be more likely to adopt that attitude themselves. You don't need to push your chill mindset onto others; just show them how much better life can be when you stop overthinking and start enjoying the ride.

Chapter 40: Remembering That Nobody's Perfect (And That's Fine)

Perfection is an illusion. No one has it all together all the time, and trying to be perfect is exhausting and ultimately unnecessary. Embracing the idea that nobody's perfect is one of the easiest ways to share chill vibes with others. When you remind your friends (and yourself) that it's okay to mess up, fall short, or not have everything figured out, you help create a more relaxed and understanding atmosphere. It's crucial to stop comparing yourself to an impossible ideal and start accepting yourself as you are. Perfectionism not only breeds stress, it also makes us less connected to the people around us. We're all flawed and that's perfectly fine—it's what makes us human. When you embrace imperfection, you invite others to do the same. The more we all accept that none of us is perfect, the easier it is to support each other and celebrate life's messy, unpredictable moments.

Chapter 41: What Does "Go With the Flow" Even Mean?

The phrase "go with the flow" is tossed around a lot these days, but what does it really mean? It sounds simple, like just kicking back and letting life happen, but there's more to it than just being passive or going along with whatever life throws at you. It's a mindset, a way of navigating through the ups and downs of life with a sense of ease, without resisting or trying to control everything. In this section, we'll break down what it means to "go with the flow," why it's not about being lazy, and how you can stop fighting life and just start riding the waves.

Chapter 42: It's Not About Being Lazy (Well, Not Totally)

One of the most common misconceptions about going with the flow is that it means doing nothing. People assume that if you're not constantly pushing, hustling, or trying to get ahead, you're just being lazy. But that's not the case. Going with the flow doesn't mean you're not putting in effort; it means that you're not rigidly attached to an outcome or fighting against the current. It's about learning how to work with life instead of against it. Life has a way of throwing unexpected twists your way—some good, some not so great—and if you're too focused on your original plans or expectations, you're going to feel frustrated every time things don't go as expected. Going with the flow means being flexible enough to adapt when things change, without completely giving up on your goals. It's not about doing nothing; it's about finding balance between effort and surrender. You don't have to be passive to go with the flow—you just have to be adaptable and willing to see where the current takes you.

Chapter 43: How to Stop Fighting Life and Just Ride the Waves

We all know the feeling of trying to force things to go our way. Whether it's stressing over schoolwork, fighting with family, or battling against the randomness of life, it's easy to get caught up in trying to control everything. The problem with that is life isn't something you can control. No matter how much you plan, no matter how hard you try, things don't always go the way you want them to. The more you fight life, the more drained and frustrated you become. So, what's the alternative? Instead of fighting the current, you can learn to ride it. It's like being in a lazy river. When you try to fight the flow, you end up exhausted and stuck in one place, but when you stop resisting and let the current take you, you start moving effortlessly forward. It doesn't mean you don't make choices or take action—it just means you stop trying to force everything into your exact vision. When you stop fighting life, you start moving with it, finding joy even in the moments you didn't expect. Life isn't always predictable, and that's okay. Learn to ride the waves, and you'll find it a lot less stressful.

Chapter 44: Why Being Chill Doesn't Mean Giving Up

Some people mistakenly think that going with the flow means you've given up, that you're not trying hard enough or taking life seriously. But that couldn't be further from the truth. Being chill doesn't mean you're not engaged with life; it means you're not letting stress, fear, or frustration take over. It's about recognizing that you can't control everything and that sometimes, the best way to handle life's challenges is with a calm and relaxed attitude. It's easy to get caught up in the rush to do more, be more, or achieve more, but constantly pushing yourself can lead to burnout and anxiety. Going with the flow is about finding a balance between effort and relaxation, between pursuing your goals and accepting that not everything is in your hands. It doesn't mean you're giving up—it means you're choosing a healthier, less stressful way of living. When you can embrace the flow of life, you can stay more centered and grounded, even when things get tough.

Chapter 45: How to Stay Chill When Life Gets Messy

Life isn't always smooth sailing. Sometimes it feels like you're stuck in a storm, and no matter how hard you try, you can't seem to get things to go your way. Whether it's a bad day at school, a fight with a friend, or just a series of unfortunate events, life can get messy. But how do you stay chill in these moments? In this section, we'll explore why freaking out never helps, how to deal with change without losing your cool, and how to find the good side of bad days.

Chapter 46: Why Freaking Out Never Solves Anything

It's easy to let panic and frustration take over when things don't go as planned. Whether it's failing a test, missing an important deadline, or dealing with unexpected drama, it's natural to want to freak out. But the truth is, freaking out never solves anything. It only adds unnecessary stress and makes it harder to think clearly. When you're caught up in a panic attack or spiraling into negative thoughts, you're not able to see your way forward. Instead of freaking out, try to take a step back, breathe, and assess the situation. Ask yourself, "What can I do right now to improve this?" Focus on taking small, manageable actions instead of getting overwhelmed by the big picture. If something bad happens, take a moment to process your emotions, but then let go of the urge to freak out. Going with the flow means responding to challenges with a clear head and a calm attitude. Freaking out might feel like it's helping, but in reality, it only makes things worse.

Chapter 47: How to Deal with Change Without Losing It

Change is inevitable, but that doesn't make it any easier. Whether it's a move to a new city, a shift in your friend group, or just a sudden change in plans, life is constantly evolving. The challenge is learning how to stay grounded when everything around you is shifting. The first step is to accept that change is part of life, and it's something we can't avoid. Instead of resisting it or wishing things were different, learn to adapt. Going with the flow doesn't mean passively accepting everything that happens to you—it means learning how to flow with it. When change happens, instead of panicking or feeling like it's the end of the world, focus on what you can control. If your plans change, adjust. If you lose something important, make space for something new. Life moves in cycles, and sometimes the best thing you can do is embrace the change rather than fighting against it. By learning to adapt and stay calm, you'll find that change becomes less intimidating, and you can handle it with more ease.

Chapter 48: Finding the Good Side of Bad Days

Bad days happen to everyone. You might get into a fight with a friend, fail a test, or just wake up feeling off. It's easy to let a bad day drag you down, but it's important to remember that even in the worst moments, there's usually something good to be found. Going with the flow means being able to find the silver lining, even on days that seem to be going wrong. Maybe you didn't get the grade you wanted, but you learned something new. Maybe you argued with your friend, but it gave you an opportunity to better understand each other. Even the worst days have something valuable in them if you're willing to look for it. Instead of focusing on what went wrong, take a moment to reflect on the positives. Maybe you took a break and went for a walk, or maybe you learned how to handle a tough situation. Going with the flow is about finding peace and gratitude in the middle of the mess. Bad days don't have to define you—they're just part of the journey.

Chapter 49: Making Chill Choices

The way we navigate through life often comes down to the choices we make. While you can't always control what happens to you, you can control how you respond to it. In this section, we'll discuss how to make more chill choices, from picking your battles wisely to avoiding unnecessary drama and learning to laugh at the weird, unexpected things life throws at you.

Chapter 50: Picking Battles That Actually Matter

In life, there will always be conflicts and challenges. But not every battle is worth fighting. One of the key elements of going with the flow is knowing when to let things slide and when to stand up for yourself. Many of the small issues we face—like a minor disagreement, a delay in plans, or an awkward moment—don't really matter in the grand scheme of things. Instead of getting worked up over every little thing, try to pick your battles. Ask yourself, "Is this really worth my energy?" If it's something that can be easily solved or something that's not going to affect you long-term, let it go. Going with the flow means being able to choose when to engage and when to just let things be. When you focus on the things that truly matter, you'll find that you can handle life with a lot more ease and calm.

- <u>Nivaan Alex</u>